BBC EARTH

planet earth
our extraordinary world

SCHOLASTIC READER

LEVEL **3**

700-1500 WORDS

PRINTED ON RECYCLED PAPER

WHO LIVES IN THE FOREST?

By Lisa L. Ryan-Herndon

SCHOLASTIC INC.

New York   Toronto   London   Auck
Sydney   Mexico City   New Delhi   Hor

BBC EARTH and PLANET EARTH are trademarks of the BBC and are used under license. PLANET EARTH logo © BBC 2006 BBC logo © 1996. Published by Scholastic Inc. SCHOLASTIC and associated logos are trademarks and/or registered trademarks of Scholastic Inc.

ISBN 978-0-545-15357-7

12 11 10 9 8 7 6 5 4 3 2 1   10 11 12 13 14/0

Printed in the U.S.A. 40

First printing, June 2010

♻ Printed on paper containing minimum of 30% post-consumer fiber.

CONTENTS

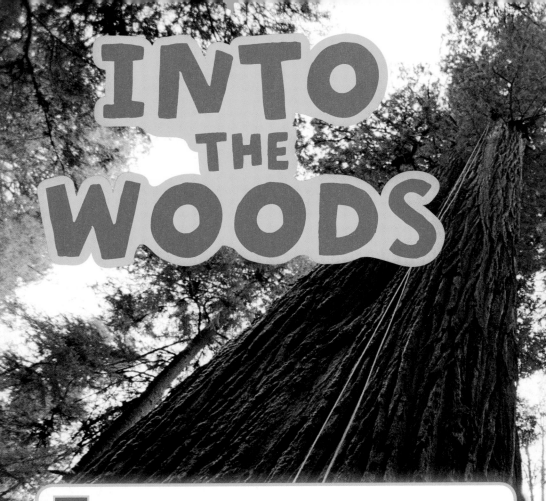

INTO THE WOODS

Trees are the largest, tallest, oldest, and most important plants on Earth. Trees recycle the air we breathe. People and animals couldn't live on this planet if there weren't any trees.

Many trees grow in **forests**. A forest is a large group of trees covering an area. Forests can grow in cold, hot, wet, or dry environments. There are two tree families; **deciduous** trees grow leaves. **Coniferous** trees grow needles and cones.

Every year, our planet makes a trip around the Sun. As it travels, we experience four different **seasons**. Winter, spring, summer, and fall bring changes in temperature and weather to forests and all other **habitats**. In forests, trees and animals change during each season.

Winter

Winter is the coldest season. Lack of sunlight means lower temperatures. Tiny rain droplets freeze and fall as snow. But the world's largest forest stays green even in the winter. A third of Earth's trees cover the **taiga**, where winter lasts 11 months! Most of the trees in the taiga are coniferous evergreens, so they are green all year long.

The taiga covers Canada, Alaska, Scandinavia, and Russia.

Many animals can't eat from coniferous trees. Needles and cones hide the tree's seeds. But the crossbill's super-long beak crosses at the tip. It works like a pry bar to open a cone and reach the hidden seeds.

CROSSBILL

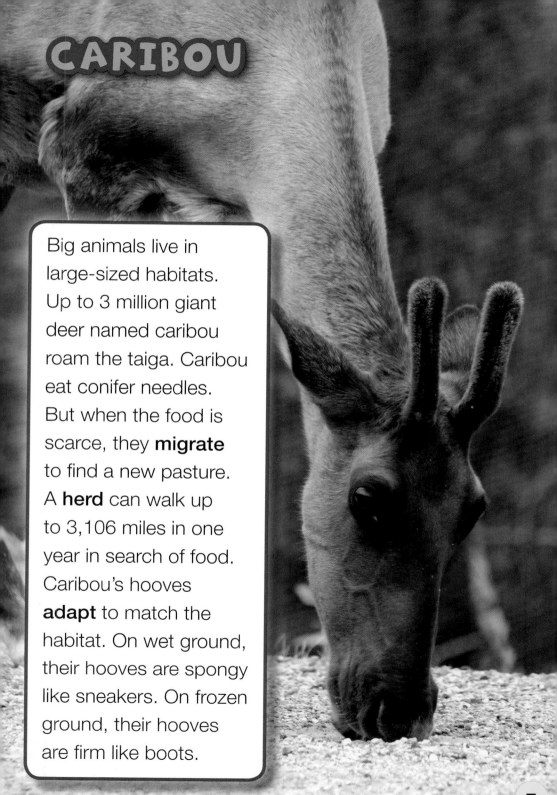

CARIBOU

Big animals live in large-sized habitats. Up to 3 million giant deer named caribou roam the taiga. Caribou eat conifer needles. But when the food is scarce, they **migrate** to find a new pasture. A **herd** can walk up to 3,106 miles in one year in search of food. Caribou's hooves **adapt** to match the habitat. On wet ground, their hooves are spongy like sneakers. On frozen ground, their hooves are firm like boots.

SNOWSHOE HARE

The snowshoe hare is named for its large, furry feet. Snowshoe hares thump their hind feet against the ground to "talk," especially when their huge ears hear trouble. Its summer coat is brown or gray. But in the winter its coat turns as white as snow, helping it hide from **predators** like the lynx.

LYNX

Thick fur, long hind legs, and big feet make the lynx perfect for hunting snowshoe hare. Lynx will also hunt mice, voles, grouse, ptarmigan, and other birds. Lynx have thick silver-colored fur coats for surviving the cold winter. In summer, their coats often become more reddish or gray-brown.

This huge weasel is more than 1 foot tall, weighs up to 40 pounds, and has jaws that are strong enough to break bones. A wolverine doesn't have to migrate because it can catch a wide range of **prey** — from mice to caribou. The wolverine is also a **scavenger**. It will steal another predator's meal, storing snacks in the snow for later.

A wolverine can smell prey 6 feet beneath the snow.

WOLVERINE

EURASIAN BLACK VULTURE

The Eurasian black vulture migrates from Asia to Eastern Russia's deciduous forest for the winter. There, the trees have lost their leaves. But that's okay for the world's largest bird of prey. It is too big to hide. This vulture can weigh up to 28 pounds and its wings stretch 8-to-10 feet wide. Surprisingly, female vultures are larger than the males. This scavenger scares predators away to steal their leftovers.

AMUR LEOPARD

Eastern Russia is also the home to the world's rarest big cat, the Amur leopard, also known as the Far Eastern leopard. Fewer than 35 Amur leopards live in the wild. This big cat grows a 3-inch-long coat to survive during the cold winter, and its long legs help it pad through the deep Siberian snow. After the leopard catches a deer, hare, or badger, it carries its meal up to the branches of a tree and eats it there.

A female Amur leopard gives birth to 1 to 4 cubs in each litter and spends up to two years rearing them.

Spring

Spring brings change. Longer days and more sunshine melt the ice and snow. Fresh water flows in the rivers again. Rain causes green buds to sprout on branches. Eggs hatch. But new life for some means more food for others.

MARBLED MURRELET

The female marbled murrelet only lays one egg per year.

North America is home to the world's tallest trees. The coniferous redwoods grow higher than 200 feet! The tallest redwood is 379 feet high. Nesting on a branch you might find the marbled murrelet, an **endangered** seabird. Mother and father murrelets take turns feeding their chicks. When chicks are ready to leave the nest for the first time, or **fledge**, they pluck out their **down**, leaving only flight feathers. At night, the birds leave the nest and fly out to sea.

Great grey owls nest high overhead in North America and Eurasia. These predators hunt day and night. Their wings flap silently as they swoop to grab mice, voles, and squirrels with their small, sharp **talons**. Both parents tend to their chicks for five months. A **fledgling** owl learns how to fly in two weeks, using its talons to climb and flap-hop between branches.

GREAT GREY OWL

PINE MARTEN

The wolverine's American cousin is the pine marten. This weasel nests in trees, but hunts on the ground at dawn and dusk. The pine marten steals bird eggs in the spring and summer. But in fall and winter, squirrels become its prey.

MANDARIN DUCK

The male mandarin duck grows colorful feathers to attract female ducks.

Mandarin ducks live near streams in Eastern Europe and Asia. A female lays 8 to 10 eggs in a tree hole 30 feet aboveground. A month later, the eggs hatch one day at a time. Their mother calls and ducklings leap from their nests to land with a bounce. Once they have all hatched, the new family waddles to their watery home.

Summer

Summer brings more sunshine and less rainfall. Deciduous trees are green with leaves. Food is easy to find. South of the equator, the sun's heat turns rain into steam. Flowers bloom. Their strong scent invites birds, bugs, and other animals to gather beneath the trees.

PUDU

In South America, the "Redwoods of the South" grow in Chile's Valdivian forests where life is miniature-sized. Alerce trees reach 165 feet high, but gunnera plants form a lower **canopy** under which the world's smallest animals walk. The pudu is a tiny deer just 12 inches tall with 4-inch-long antlers. Its fawns are the size of kittens.

MONITO DEL MONTE

The monito del monte is a **marsupial** that looks like a mouse. It uses its tail to climb among the gunnera. Scientists call the monito del monte a "living fossil" because it is the only living member of a species dating back 40 million years! This nighttime hunter eats bugs, frogs, and mistletoe berries.

Babies stay in a mother's pouch for two months.

KODKOD CAT

South America's smallest wildcat, the kodkod cat, is smaller and more mysterious than a house cat. Despite its small size, this wildcat is a keen hunter, preying on monito and pudu during the night.

LANGUR MONKEY AND CHITAL DEER

Summer is more like fall in India's teak forest. Most deciduous trees shed leaves to store water in their bark. But the mahua tree blooms in May. Many animal species drink its flowers' **nectar**. The langur monkey and chital deer share a "buddy system" when feeding. In the branches, monkeys knock down flowers to the deer below. The deer alert the monkeys if a tiger is coming.

BENGAL TIGER

There are currently between 3 and 5 thousand Bengal tigers living in the Indian sub-continent.

Bengal tigers live in India and are sometimes called Indian tigers. This predator roams many habitats, but hunts best under a forest's cover. Mother tigers raise cubs for 15 months, and then they go on to hunt alone. Tigers like water and can swim great distances. The Bengal can weigh more than 500 pounds and eat up to 40 pounds in one meal. Its roar can be heard from 2 miles away.

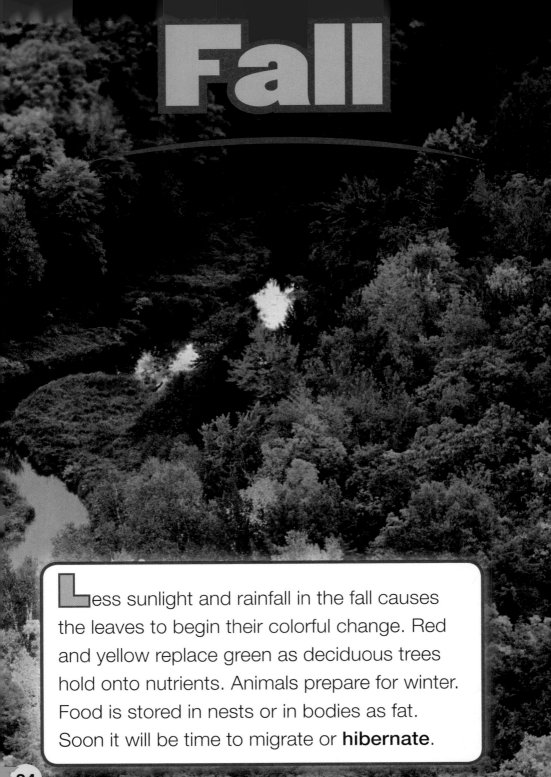

Fall

Less sunlight and rainfall in the fall causes the leaves to begin their colorful change. Red and yellow replace green as deciduous trees hold onto nutrients. Animals prepare for winter. Food is stored in nests or in bodies as fat. Soon it will be time to migrate or **hibernate**.

HAWK MOTH AND MOUSE LEMUR

On the island of Madagascar, baobab trees store more than 31,000 gallons of water inside their 22-foot-wide trunks. At night, foot-long flowers bloom. Its nectar is a treat for animals from hawk moths to mouse lemurs. When the giant hawk moth drinks nectar, its body transfers pollen between flowers. Lemurs also **pollinate** while catching moths to store body fat for the long winter.

CICADA

A deciduous forest is the base of the food chain.
Mammals eat insects and birds, which feed on
bugs, which eat leaves from the forest. Cicadas
are bugs that live underground for 17 years until
one night when a trillion of them burst upward
and swarm the forest. For 10 days, cicadas sing,
eat, lay eggs, and then die, leaving food for their
predators.

RACCOON

Raccoons will wash food in nearby water before eating it.

This "masked bandit" lives in forests and cities around the world. Raccoons can adapt to many environments. They nest in trees or hollow logs. As nighttime hunters, they eat everything — berries, bugs (like cicada), fish, small mammals such as mice, and eggs. Raccoons don't hibernate and continue to search for food throughout the winter.

CLARK'S NUTCRACKER

Frost hardens the ground. In the taiga forests of the Northern Hemisphere, a bird called the Clark's nutcracker hides whitebark pine nuts in the ground before it freezes. It hides 30,000 nuts every year in 5,000 different places! In spring this bird uses its amazing memory to find most of the stored nuts. The nuts that are not found grow into new pine trees. In this way, the trees and birds need each other to survive.

BACK
TO THE
BEGINNING

The end of one season brings the beginning of the next. Trees flourish in all seasons and in all parts of the world. Trees share air and life with every creature on planet Earth.

GLOSSARY

adapt – to change in body or behavior to survive changes in an environment.

canopy – the top area of a tree.

coniferous – an evergreen tree that grows needles and cones (examples: fir, spruce, and pine).

deciduous – a tree that grows and sheds leaves (examples: birch, beech, aspen, and maple).

down – a bird's soft, fluffy feathers.

endangered – a species of animal or plant that is in danger of dying out.

fledge – when a baby bird is ready to fly.

fledgling – a young bird.

forest – a large area thickly covered with trees.

habitat – the place where an animal lives.

herd – a large group of animals.

hibernate – to sleep during the winter season.

marsupial – a mammal with a pouch.

migrate – to move from one place to another.

nectar – a sweet liquid from a plant.

pollinate – to move pollen between flowers, causing them to reproduce.

predators - animals that hunt other animals for food.

prey – an animal that is hunted by other animals for food.

scavenger – an animal that will eat the remains of another animal's meals.

season – one of the four natural parts of the year.

taiga – the world's largest forest spans Russia, Canada, Alaska, and Scandinavia for a total distance of 1.5 million square miles.

talons – claws shaped like a hook.

THERE IS ONLY ONE PLANET EARTH

The trees in our forests are important! Trees help keep our air clean, improve water quality, and save energy. Plant a tree today!

Remember the Three R's. Reduce. Reuse. Recycle.

BBC EARTH

www.bbcearth.com